CONTENTS

THE CITY OF LONDON

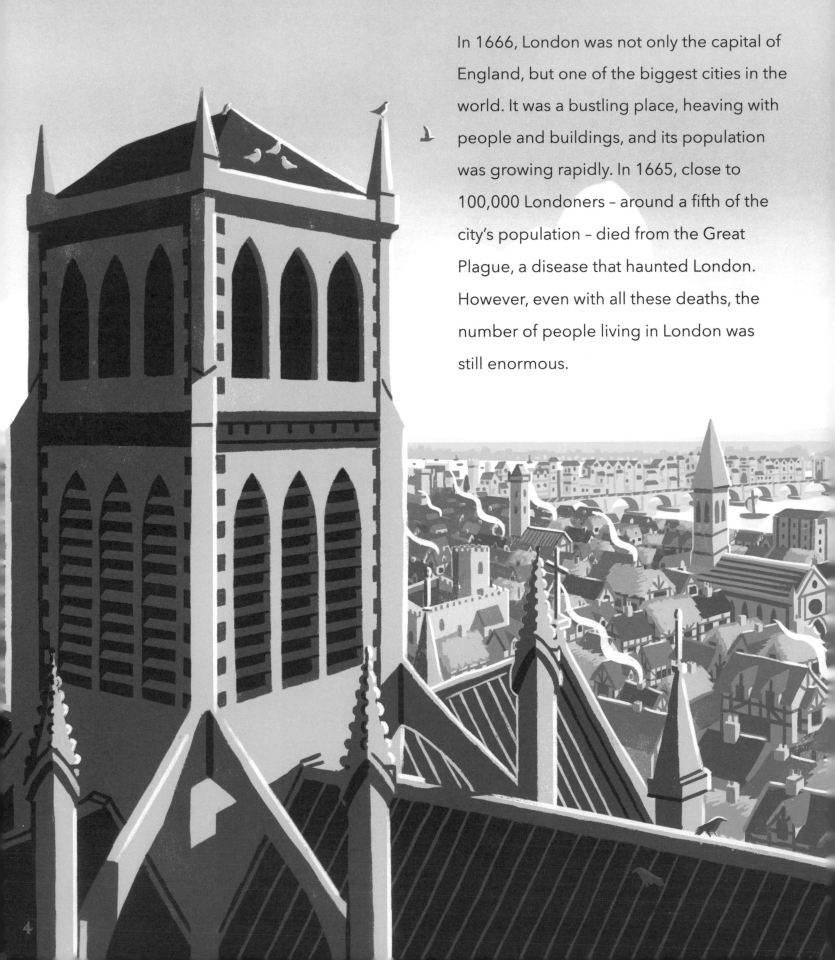

In 1666, London was not only the capital of England, but one of the biggest cities in the world. It was a bustling place, heaving with people and buildings, and its population was growing rapidly. In 1665, close to 100,000 Londoners – around a fifth of the city's population – died from the Great Plague, a disease that haunted London. However, even with all these deaths, the number of people living in London was still enormous.

Ple

THE
GREAT
FIRE
OF
LONDON

Emma Adams

James Weston Lewis

WAYLAND

London's burning,

London's burning,

Fire, fire!

Fire, fire!

And in 1666, the city was very different
from the one we know today.

5

Buildings were mostly made from wood, straw and a tar-like substance called pitch, which protected the wood from water damage. However, the pitch also caught fire easily …

In the poorest parts of London, the buildings were so close together that neighbours could lean out of their own home and touch the house opposite. And the smell! Horse-drawn carts and carriages were pulled along the cobbled streets, and animal mess mixed with the waste from houses. There were few street sweepers, and no sewer systems to keep the city clean.

London was very noisy,
very busy and very dirty.

A LONG, HOT SUMMER

London experienced an especially hot summer that year. In fact, very little rain had fallen across the whole of southern England. Buildings dried out, the ground became dusty and even London's main river, the Thames, was running low from so little rainfall.

There was no electricity to light or heat homes, so fire was an essential part of life. Families would build open fires in their houses to keep them warm and to cook meals. When night fell, they would put out the roaring flames and light candles to see by. So people needed fire to survive – but fire could be dangerous in a crowded city like London.

THOMAS FARRINER'S BAKERY

Thomas Farriner owned a busy bakery on Pudding Lane, in east London. He was the baker to Charles II, the king at that time. The large stone oven in the bakery was lit in the early hours of each morning and burned throughout the day. At night, as the bakery was closing, the flames were beaten down to ashes. But on Saturday 1st September 1666, no one made sure that the fire in Farriner's bakery had been properly put out. The oven continued to burn, and no one noticed . . .

SUNDAY
2ND SEPTEMBER

In the early hours of Sunday morning, the Great Fire of London started. Some say it was because a hot ember fell from the oven and set fire to a nearby pile of wood. Others say that Farriner had forgotten to sweep out the oven, which meant that the dying fire sprang back to life. Even Farriner's maid was blamed – although she never had the chance to deny this, because she was one of the first people to be killed by the fire.

By 3 o'clock in the morning, flames rose high above Pudding Lane and could be seen from a quarter of a mile away. A strong wind helped the fire move quickly, blowing it west from house to house. It fed off the dry wooden frames of buildings and licked at thatched roofs and pitch, pushing southwards towards London Bridge. If the fire travelled across the bridge, everyone and everything south of the river would also be in great danger.

PEPYS' DIARY

Samuel Pepys is now famous for the diary he kept between 1660 and 1669. He was a highly regarded Londoner because he worked as an administrator in the Navy, and later became a Member of Parliament. Pepys' diary is more than a million words long and is packed with detail about his personal life and work. It also contains information on great moments in British history, such as the coronation of King Charles II, the devastation of the Great Plague and, of course, the Great Fire of London.

In his diary, Pepys wrote that his maid rushed to tell him about the spreading fire.

> "By and by Jane comes and tells me that she hears that above 300 houses have been burned down to-night by the fire we saw, and that it is now burning down all Fish-street, by London Bridge."

– The Diary of Samuel Pepys

The only way to stop the fire from spreading was to create a firebreak – houses had to be pulled down to create space between the fire and the buildings still standing. Most people didn't want to tear down their homes, but nothing else would stop the fire. Pepys went to King Charles and asked him to take action. The King was deeply troubled by Pepys' visit and sent him to deliver his message to the Lord Mayor of London, Sir Thomas Bludworth. The Mayor was sent into a panic, shouting **"Lord! What can I do? . . . I have been pulling down houses; but the fire overtakes us faster than we can do it."**

The fire continued to spread west towards Thames Street, to warehouses filled with oil and alcohol. This deadly combination fed the flames and made the fire even more dangerous.

MONDAY 3RD SEPTEMBER

Only a day after the first flames had escaped the oven, the Great Fire was unstoppable. It raged through the city, destroying some of the buildings on London Bridge. By evening, the flames burned so brightly that night looked like day, and ash fell from the sky like snow.

TUESDAY
4TH SEPTEMBER

By Tuesday, the fire was so hot that nobody could get close enough to fight it. The firefighting equipment was no match for the blaze. And when St Paul's Cathedral caught fire, and Ludgate Hill and part of Fleet Street went up in flames, King Charles II ordered that as many buildings as possible be knocked down. Men, women and children fled their homes, taking as much with them as they could carry, even burying some of their belongings to protect them.

Some people escaped on foot, in carts and by boat, while others stayed to fight the fire. At its worst point, the Great Fire of London burnt through 100 houses in just one hour. But thankfully the strong winds were starting to weaken.

WEDNESDAY 5TH SEPTEMBER

On Wednesday, the smell of gunpowder filled the air as houses and shops were blown up. Many important buildings, including St Paul's Cathedral, the Royal Exchange and Guildhall, couldn't be saved from the fire.

The King took charge of the firefighting, and organised groups of people to demolish buildings. Lines of men snaked from the River Thames to riverside houses and shops that were still on fire, passing buckets of water between them. It was a slow process, but the biggest flames began to die down. More than three days after it had started, the Great Fire was finally under control.

"Lord! what sad sight it was by moone-light to see, the whole City almost on fire."

– *The Diary of Samuel Pepys*

A City In Ruins

Once all of the flames were put out, east London was unrecognisable. Around 400 streets had been burnt to the ground, 87 churches lay in ruins and more than 13,000 houses were reduced to ashes. Amazingly, it was reported that fewer than ten people had died in the fire. Most had escaped to the fields north of the city.

It was in those fields - in Moorfields, Highgate and Islington - that the rich and poor set up tents and huts beside each other. Pepys was surprised to see that some wealthy people had chosen to save their musical instruments from the fire.

South of the River Thames was safe. London could be rebuilt.

King Charles II wanted to create a grand new city that would be the envy of Europe, with wide streets, beautiful parks and no over-crowding. But there just wasn't enough money for the King's dream to be realised. Tradesmen needed to re-open their businesses quickly and families needed their homes to be rebuilt cheaply.

In 1668, two years after the Great Fire, new rules were put in place meaning that buildings had to stand further apart from each other and be made from brick and stone, instead of wood and straw. It would take 30 years for London to be rebuilt properly. In 1669, the architect Christopher Wren designed a brand-new St Paul's Cathedral. Although it took almost 40 years for the cathedral to be completed, it still stands proudly in London today.

CHANGES TO FIREFIGHTING

Before the Great Fire, firefighting methods were very basic.

People used leather buckets and hand squirts filled with water – but it was hard to get hold of the equipment because there wasn't enough to go around.

After the Great Fire, new and improved techniques were put in place.

London was divided into four areas, each with its own firefighting service and equipment.

Hand-pulled fire engines were rare but were introduced slowly, and by the 18th century, horse-drawn fire engines could be seen on London's streets.

By 1832, there were 15 separate fire brigades in London and, because firefighting was still difficult to organise, they joined together to create what would eventually become known as the London Fire Brigade.

The brigade had 77 firefighters,

14 fire engines . . .

and 13 fire stations.

IN MEMORY

Between 1671 and 1677, a memorial to the Great Fire was built. Designed by Christopher Wren and Robert Hooke, it is 61.5 metres tall and, at the junction of Monument Street and Fish Street Hill, it stands exactly 61.5 metres away from where the fire began on Pudding Lane. It is called the Monument.

PEOPLE

KING CHARLES II

(29th May 1630 – 6th February 1685)
Son of King Charles I

Charles II became King of England, Scotland and Ireland in 1649 but spent 11 years in exile and only returned to Britain in 1660. His coronation took place on 23rd April 1661 at Westminster Abbey.

SIR THOMAS BLUDWORTH

(Baptised 13th February 1620 – 12th May 1682)
Merchant and politician

Sir Thomas Bludworth was the Lord Mayor of London from October 1665 to October 1666. At first, he thought the Great Fire of London was no real threat, and so was reluctant to knock down buildings. Many people thought this was the reason the fire caused so much damage. In Pepys' diary, he calls Bludworth "a silly man".

SAMUEL PEPYS

(23rd February 1633 – 26th May 1703)
Naval administrator and Member of Parliament

Samuel Pepys was a respected man at the time of the Great Fire. Through hard work, public support and his natural talent for administration, he rose through the ranks in the Navy and became Chief Secretary to the Admiralty. His diary gives a first-hand account of many important events in British history, including the Great Plague and the Great Fire.

PLACES

ST PAUL'S CATHEDRAL

When the old St Paul's Cathedral was burnt to the ground during the Great Fire of London, the architect Christopher Wren designed a new cathedral to stand in its place. It took almost 40 years to build, but that cathedral still stands today. It even survived the bombs falling on London during the Blitz of the Second World War.

LONDON BRIDGE

For many years, London Bridge was the only bridge in London to cross the River Thames. At the time of the Great Fire, it was lined with around 200 buildings and was actually built in a different place – a whole 30 metres east – from where it is today.

OLD BAILEY

The Central Criminal Court is known as the Old Bailey, after the street it stands on. It is one of a number of buildings that house the Crown Court, and it was destroyed in the Great Fire. The Old Bailey was bombed during the Second World War, and sustained severe damage. It has been restored, rebuilt and extended many times over the years.

GUILDHALL

The term "Guildhall" refers to both the building itself and its main room, the Great Hall, which was damaged during the Great Fire. Guildhall has been restored and extended over the years. A new entrance was added in 1788, new roofs were built in 1866 and 1954, and an art gallery was installed in the 1990s.

N
W E
S

SMITH FIELD

GATE STREET

CRIPPLE

ALDERS

WOOD STREET

HOLBORN

SHOE LANE

NEWGATE STREET

CHE

FLEET STREET

LUDGATE HILL

ST. PAUL'S

CARTER LANE

SALISBURY COURT

BLACK FRYERS

OLD FISH

BAYNARD'S CASTLE

THE RIVER THAMES

For my family – Emma

For Isaac, with special thanks to
Chloe, Rob, Tom and my family
– James

First published in 2016 by Wayland
Copyright © Wayland 2016
All rights reserved.

Commissioning editor: Debbie Foy
Editors: Fiz Osborne and Elizabeth Brent
Designer: Claire Yeo
Consultant: John Miles

ISBN 978 0 7502 9820 9
Printed in China
10 9 8 7 6 5 4 3 2 1

Wayland, an imprint of Hachette Children's Group
Part of Hodder and Stoughton
Carmelite House
50 Victoria Embankment
London
EC4Y 0DZ

An Hachette UK Company
www.hachette.co.uk
www.hachettechildrens.co.uk